A Survivor's Guide to
SURVIVING SEPARATION

*how to navigate a separation in Ontario,
Canada, for Family Court first-timers and
survivors of domestic violence*

Heather D. Alexander, BAH, MA, JD

this book is dedicated to
every person whose abuser
tried to destroy them

you are not alone

a better life is possible

they will not win

the information in this book is for everyone
regardless of sex or gender identity

this is not legal or medical advice

for specific legal advice, contact a lawyer
competent in family law in
your jurisdiction

for specific medical advice,
speak to your doctor

the following discussion is based on the
Ontario, Canada, family law system and is
provided for discussion
purposes only

Table of Contents

Introduction

Step One

Step Two

Step Three

Step Four

Step Five

Introduction

My name is Heather and I am a family lawyer specializing in high-conflict separations. I am also a survivor of domestic violence myself.

One of the biggest barriers to leaving a toxic relationship is not knowing what's next. This is because most people don't know what court involves. They worry that it will be expensive, out of their control, and scary.

I have written this book to help survivors and Family Court first-timers learn what your options are following separation, to take the fear out of the process, to help reduce your legal costs, and to process the end of your relationship as you heal from it.

Step one is taking care of yourself. Step two is understanding the legal issues. Step Three is identifying ways to resolve them. Step four is collecting relevant information so you can build a strong case and save money. Step five is believing that a better life is possible.

This book is designed to help you get through each step and to start your case with knowledge, confidence, & courage.

first things first

how are you feeling?
be honest.

let me tell you something

my story.

I worked hard my entire life.

I wasn't from money, so I put myself through law
school with loans, graduated at the top of my class,
and developed a promising career at a great firm.

Everything was going well, except I did not have love.

Then _he_ found me.

He was tall, dark and handsome with a southern accent, and he found me
online, through our shared love of music. I had posted a cover of my
favourite song on
YouTube, and he commented:

"I do a cover myself, but yours is much better."

We struck up a quick friendship, and then something more. Within the
first few weeks he was talking about marriage. It seemed crazy, but he
swore that he was my soul mate.

It was a cosmic connection - a once in a lifetime love.

He would propose to me twice over the time I knew him. He would also
deceive and manipulate me shamelessly, lying through his teeth to my
face.

Being with him made me feel alive in a way I never had before. He just _got_
me. But he also physically assaulted me, psychologically tormented me,
stole, cheated, and lied.

When I finally left, I wanted to die. I loved him more than anything, but I
knew that I could not trust him.

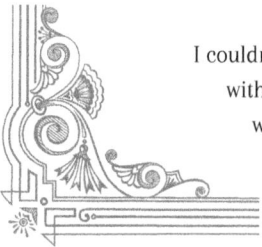

I couldn't live like that - but I couldn't live
without him, either. Soon, the only
way I could fall asleep was by
imagining I was dead.

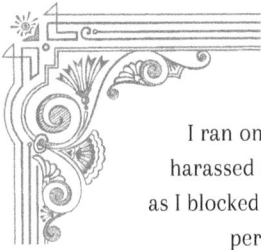

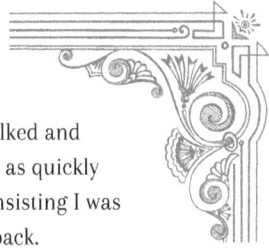

I ran on fumes for weeks as he stalked and
harassed me, creating new accounts as quickly
as I blocked them, swearing his love, insisting I was
perfect, begging me to come back.

Every day got harder. I couldn't breathe. I couldn't sleep.
I developed stress rashes. I felt like a zombie.

One day, I went to the office for 7:30 a.m. like normal. I sat down at my
desk and the next thing I knew, it was 9:45 a.m. My alarm was
going off. I needed to be in court for 10 a.m.

I had lost over two hours of time. This was my first
experience with dissociation.

I stood up but it felt like I was under water. I couldn't think straight. My
heart was pounding out of my chest and my lungs seared with pain. I
began hyperventilating. The memories, promises, and dreams of our
future tore at me mercilessly like wild dogs, except the
pain was coming from the inside, out.

That morning I pulled it together, went to court,
and then walked off my job forever.

That was the start of my mental breakdown. It was not just one stressful
day. It was a turning point following years of psychological, emotional,
physical and financial torture. It changed my brain.
It changed my entire life.

I was taken off work by my doctor. I had to sell my
house to pay my student loans. I lost my love, my
home, my career and my mental health all
at once.

But worst of all, I lost all hope.

My abuser had destroyed my life. I no hope for a better future, so I decided to write down everything he had done to me, and then I would sewer slide.

The thing is, a book about your own trauma is retraumatizing, and therefore takes forever to write. I tried psychiatry and therapy but neither helped, so I gave up on the idea of treatment, and lived in a world of extraordinary pain for years.

Looking back, I'm still not sure how I survived that.

But if you know anything about me, you know that I am tenacious, and I believe in justice. Since there was no legal penalty for emotional and psychological abuse, I knew I needed to make my own by telling my truth - loudly.

I could not die without writing everything down, because then he would get away with what he had done.

So I lived on, and to my great luck, finally got in with a fantastic psychiatrist. This is the point where my life changed again - this time for good.

I was diagnosed with complex PTSD, anxiety, depression and OCD from the abuse. I started a treatment plan combining talk therapy with a mild anti-depressant.

Two years later, I am healthier than ever. I love myself. I understand what survivors are going through, and I understand how abusers think.

My psychiatrist says that I was incredibly sick, but I didn't realize how sick I was when I was going through it.

...and this is why I'm telling you my story.

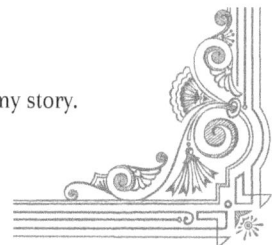

When I was at my worst, I sold or gave
away everything I owned. That made putting
my life back together much more difficult.

If you are tired of trying -
If you feel like giving up -
If your happiness is gone -

This is not the end.
You can get better.
You can find **real** happiness.

<u>The first step is to love yourself.</u>

Pick up the phone and call your doctor.
Tell them what you are going through and how you feel.

Ask for a psychiatric referral. If you don't like your first
psychiatrist, ask for a referral to someone new.

Try therapy. If you don't connect with your
first therapist, try someone new.

Consider specialized trauma, grief therapy, EMDR or somatic
therapy. Ask about other options.

Care for your body. Eat a balanced diet. Feel your pain and
work through it. Cut back on depressants like alcohol.
Go for walks. Be in nature.

Plan for **your life**, not for your death, like I did.

Most important, talk to your doctor and a family lawyer
before you sell all of your worldly possessions.
You don't have to start over from scratch.

You can get through this, and
I wrote this book to show you how to start.

STEP ONE

assess and keep track of your health

THE IMPORTANCE OF *diagnosis*

when I finally left my abuser, I was in the midst of a mental health crisis that he had caused

Does this sound familiar to you?

If you are feeling unwell physically or mentally, please put down this book and make an appointment with your family doctor, psychiatrist or therapist immediately.

Be honest about what has been happening in your life. Keep in mind that mental health issues may express as physical ailments. For example, my anxiety first expressed as an inability to breathe, and later as a skin rash. Your doctor may be able to diagnose mysterious physical ailments as a part of a larger condition.

If you suspect that you need mental health assistance, ask your doctor for a referral for a Psychiatric Assessment and therapy.

Obtain a diagnosis & follow the treatment plan

The legal system respects medical diagnoses.
This is especially important if your physical or mental health is impacting your ability to parent or to work. Not only will this help you to feel better, but this will be relevant to your legal case later.

If you are feeling like harming yourself or harming someone else, contact 911 immediately.

THE IMPORTANCE OF *therapy*

Over the years, I have noticed that many people will
come in to my office, start talking and...

EVERYTHING comes out.

These folks have never discussed their
relationship with anyone.

I stop them kindly and tell them that while these things are
important to them, some are better sorted through
with a qualified therapist.

I then ask for permission to direct the topics of our meeting so
that I can keep our discussions relevant and keep their
costs as low as possible.

As a lawyer, I understand that this is a better use
of their budget and time.

However, as a survivor, I appreciate the importance of talking
about what happened to you. Working through it. Receiving
validation that it was horrific and wrong.

If you don't have a therapist, get one.

Keep track of how you are feeling throughout the separation
process using the following **daily wellness journal**, and
share it with your care providers.

Knowledge truly is power, especially in
your healing journey.

JOURNAL OPTION #1

IS VERY SIMPLE - IF YOU DON'T FEEL UP TO JOURNALING,
THIS OPTION ALLOWS YOU TO KEEP TRACK OF HOW YOU
FEEL USING A 1-10 KEY

JOURNAL OPTION #2

IS SLIGHTLY MORE INVOLVED - THIS OPTION ENCOURAGES
YOU TO INCORPORATE A POSITIVE OUTLOOK INTO YOUR
DAILY PERSPECTIVE WHICH CAN ASSIST WITH
REFRAMING AND, ULTIMATELY, HEALING

JOURNAL OPTION #3

THIS OPTION ALLOWS YOU TO JOURNAL SEAMLESSLY WITH
NO RESTRICTIONS OR BARRIERS AND IS INTENDED FOR USE
ALONG WITH OPTIONS 1 AND 2

WELLNESS
JOURNAL

Date:

1 - 2 - 3 - 4 - 5 - 6 - 7 - 8 - 9 - 10
1 = worst and 10 = best

How does my body feel at this moment?

How does my heart feel at this moment?

How does my head feel at this moment?

YOU BELONG

What do I need to talk about?

DAILY WELLNESS LOG

DATE

DAILY AFFIRMATION

WATER TRACKER   ⬡⬡⬡⬡⬡⬡⬡

EXERCISE LOG

MOOD TRACKER   😖 😟 😐 🙂 😊

TODAY I AM GRATEFUL FOR:

MEALS

1.

BREAKFAST

LUNCH

2.

DINNER

SNACKS

3.

DRINKS

THINGS I CAN DO TO MAKE TODAY GREAT:

THREE GREAT THINGS THAT HAPPENED TODAY:

1.

1.

2.

2.

3.

3.

THOUGHTS & REFLECTIONS:

MY WELLNESS JOURNAL

TIP: change their contact name in your phone to
Do Not Answer, and DO NOT ANSWER any
text about your relationship

I *don't know who needs
to hear this, but...
you will* NOT *find
validation from
your ex.*

DO answer questions related to parenting or
reasonable attempts to resolve the legal issues
unless you have lawyers, in which case the lawyers
should handle those discussions to give you peace

This was never what I wanted

A big thing I needed to make peace with in my recovery were the intrusive thoughts.

Me: why should I have to deal with all of this pain when it was never my choice to end up here?

It is important to deal with these thoughts with the assistance of a doctor, psychiatrist, or therapist.

But let me tell you a little secret that my trauma therapist shared with me - if you are alone and unequipped to deal with these feelings at this exact moment, it is okay to put them into a metaphorical "box" and to place them on a shelf until your next session with your therapist.

Give yourself permission not to suffer.

You do not have to solve the problem right now, but do not let it sit for too long.

If you are experiencing suicidal or homicidal ideation, contact emergency crisis support ASAP.

But let's look at the positives (vom - I know) but if you take me seriously, you are now in a position to reduce the pain you will feel going forward. So...

WHERE DO I GO FROM HERE?

I guess it's over

ugh

there are two types of survivors in the world - the ones who can't accept it's over, and the ones who are already done grieving by the time of the breakup

So what's next?

An out of court settlement?
Mediation? Negotiation? Arbitration?
What is the difference?

How do you get a Separation Agreement?
Is that in court or out of court?

Should I go to court? I heard that's expensive...
Do I really need a Court Order to resolve things?

How do you decide when yout heart is broken
and you don't know a thing about family law?

so what's next?

In the next section I will provide you with a basic family law primer, an overview of out-of-court settlement options, and an understanding of how a family law case is usually structured in the Ontario courts.

This is intended to help you understand some of the basic concepts, the options open to you, and what it means to "go to court" so that it is less scary.

Keep in mind that the family law is very complex, so this is just a high-level overview.

Once you have finished reading this book and have learned my cost-saving tips, consult with a lawyer you trust to get advice on your specific situation.

STEP TWO

identifying the legal issues

YOUR ♥ FAMILY LAW PRIMER

How do I get a legal separation?

This is THE most common first question I get from new clients, and the answer might surprise you.

In Canada, there is no special process to obtain a "legal separation."

You are separated when one person tells the other that the relationship is over, and there is no physical intimacy or further attempt to reconcile.

You can live "separate yet apart" in the same house or apartment.

All that it takes to achieve a "legal separation" in Ontario is to tell your ex-partner that the relationship is over.

This day becomes your **"date of separation."**

What is the difference between a separation and a Divorce Order?

Canada has laws against bigamy. **Bigamy** means being married to more than one person at a time. As a result, you need a **Divorce Order** from a court to remarry.

You may apply to the court for a Divorce Order immediately following your separation if you can prove domestic violence or infidelity. However, you will have to serve the affair partner and/or outline the abuse with proof, which can increase conflict and cost.

All separated married people have a right to bring a **Divorce Application** after living "separate and apart" for one year. This may be the better approach since it is less expensive and less likely to fan the flames of conflict.

Obtaining a Divorce Order does not resolve any of the other issues on separation. Judges often insist on seeing proof that you have resolved the other issues before they will sign off on it.

For this reason, obtaining a Divorce Order is generally a last step in resolving the issues that arise on separation.

major issues To resolve:

Child-Related Issues:

Custody a.k.a decision-making - in Canada, "custody" refers to making major decisions for the child regarding education, healthcare, religious or spiritual training, cultural training, and major extra-curricular activities. Sole or joint custody are the typical arrangements, however creative variations are possible.

Residential schedule and parenting time - this refers to where the child will live and on what schedule.

Child support - refers to the monthly support payable based on the non-residential parent's annual income and the number of children. Child support is not taxable.

"Set-off" child support - if the children share parenting time with each party for at least 40% of the month, a reduced "set-off" of child support is payable. In other words, we figure out what each parent would pay to the other, and the higher-income earned pays the lower income-earner the difference.

Section 7 or "extraordinary" expenses - are the expenses specific to that individual child (i.e. child care, extracurricular expenses, medical expenses that are not covered by benefits, post-secondary expenses, etc). These are typically shared by the parents in proportion to their respective incomes.

Relocation limitations - impose limits on where parties can move so the parenting schedule works long-term.

*** *this is not an exhaustive list***

The Best Interests of the Child Test:

In making determinations regarding custody and residence, the court will consider what is in the child's best interest in the situation.

Section 16(2) of the **Divorce Act** states that the court shall give primary consideration to the child's physical, emotional, and psychological safety, security and well-being.

The "Best Interests of the Child Test" is outlined at section 24(3) of the **Children's Law Reform Act:**

- the child's needs, given their age and stage of development, including the need for stability;
- the nature and strength of the child's relationship with each parent, family, and others who play an important role in the child's life;
- each parent's willingness to support the child's relationship with the other parent;
- the history of care of the child;
- the child's views and preferences, giving weight to the child's age and maturity;
- the child's cultural, linguistic, religious and spiritual upbringing and heritage;
- the ability and willingness of each person to care for and meet the needs of the child;
- the ability and willingness of the parents to communicate. and co-operate on matters affecting the child;
- any family violence; and
- any civil or criminal proceeding, order, condition, or measure that is relevant to the safety, security and well-being of the child.

major issues to resolve:

Financial Issues:

If you were married or common-law, the person who earns less may have a claim for **spousal support**.

Spousal support can be **compensatory** i.e. paying you back for opportunities you lost (for example, if you were a stay-at-home parent for any period of time), or **non-compensatory** i.e. correcting financial inequality (for example, if your partner is wealthy and you suffer a reduced quality of life after separation).

The recipient is generally entitled to spousal support for one-half to the full length of the relationship, provided they do not **cohabit with a new partner**, gain financial independence, etc. So if you cohabited for 15 years, you could receive spousal support for 7.5 to 15 years.

How do we calculate the length of the relationship?

We start at the **date of cohabitation** (when you began living together) and end at the **date of separation**.

You may qualify for less support if the relationship was under 5 years, or for "**indefinite term support**" if it was over 20 years, i.e. no hard end point.

If you qualify for the "**Rule of 65**" (your age plus the length of your relationship is 65 or more) you may be entitled to indefinite support with a shorter relationship.

Spousal support is taxable and must be reported to the CRA. The payor will receive a tax refund as it is paid out of after-tax money. The recipient will pay income tax.

major issues To resolve:

Financial Issues:

If you were **common-law,** but you contributed to your ex's business, or to a property or other asset held in their sole name, you may be able to claim a portion of the increase in value under "**unjust enrichment.**"

In other words, if you are not compensated then they would unfairly gain $ based on your efforts.

Equalization: If you were married, you are entitled to "equalize" what each of you accumulated during the relationship, so that you both receive 1/2 of what you amassed while together. This can be a complex process requiring specialized accountants and appraisals.

Note: **pensions** are subject to splitting using forms submitted to the pension plan administrator.

If you or your partner owned the home you lived in during marriage, it is deemed to be a "**matrimonial home**" regardless of who is on title. You each have a presumptive right to half of the value of the home from the date of marriage forward, regardless of who contributed to the cost.

If your ex refuses to leave the matrimonial home, you can ask for an order for "**exclusive possession**" pending settlement. You have a strong claim if you are the primary caregiver seeking stability of residence for the children. You may eventually need to sell or refinance so both parties can walk away with their equalization.

major issues to resolve:

The family court is empowered to make many other orders, depending on your specific situation, including:

- non-harassment;
- restraining;
- supervised access;
- parenting coordinator to assist in resolving parenting issues;
- freezing assets if you think your ex will dispose of property to hide it from you;
- life insurance to secure support orders;
- defining which expenses constitute section 7 expenses to avoid future conflict and assist with enforcement;
- pension, CPP, RRSP and other transfers required to fulfill equalization;
- interim disbursements (requiring the well-off party to pay the other's court fees so that they can access justice in the courts);
- future financial disclosure;
- reassessment of child support and s. 7 expenses. in the future;
- Family Responsibility Office enforcement of support orders;
- costs (be advised that full recovery is unlikely);
- pre-judgment interest; and
- other.

Consult with a family lawyer in your jurisdiction to find out what other relief is appropriate in your situation.

attention
SURVIVORS
the next page is extremely important

Tort of Family Violence

In 2022, the ground-breaking decision in
Ahluwalia v. Ahluwalia 2022 ONSC 1303 was released.

This case establishes the new tort of "**family violence**" which
allows survivors of domestic violence to seek monetary
damages against their abuser within a
family law proceeding.

A survivor will need to prove they were in a family
relationship and that the abuser's
conduct was:

1.   violent or threatening;
2.   a pattern of coercive and controlling behaviour; and
3. caused the plaintiff to fear for their safety and
that of another person (i.e. a child).

You will need to provide specific examples of:
physical abuse, forcible confinement, sexual abuse, threats,
harassment, stalking, failure to provide the necessaries of life,
psychological abuse, financial abuse, or killing or harming
an animal or property.

Do your best to collect police or medical reports, photos,
screen shots, documents, contemporaneous
messages with the abuser or others, witness
statements, and other concrete
evidence proving the abuse.

Tort of Family Violence

Justice Mandhane at paragraph 66 wrote:

"The harms associated with family violence include acute and chronic health issues (i.e. soft-tissue injuries, broken bones, chronic pain); mental, psychological, and social problems (i.e. low self-esteem, depression, anxiety, PTSD), underemployment and absenteeism, low career advancement, substance abuse, self-harm, suicidal ideation, death by suicide, and femicide. Physical and mental injuries, future case costs, and lost earning potential are regularly quantified in other civil law contexts. An award of spousal support will be insufficient to compensate for the true harms and financial barriers associated with family violence."

This case emphasizes the importance of providing detailed, specific examples of family violence in your materials. For survivors, this means that fulsome disclosure of abuse with documentary or other proof is of key importance.

The damages award in this case was $150,000.00.

This is a developing area of law.

Make sure to consult with a qualified family lawyer to learn about updates in the case law since the time of writing as they could impact your claim.

STEP THREE

different ways to resolve your legal issues

HOW DO I START?

Well, the first thing you need to do is decide whether to try to negotiate out of court, or whether to start a court case. Think about whether your ex was abusive, or if there was a power imbalance in the relationship. If your ex was abusive, they are more likely to delay and to disrespect or pull out of voluntary processes. You're better off in court where a Judge can supervise.

DATE OF COHABITATION

↓

DATE OF MARRIAGE

↓

DATE OF SEPARATION

↓

YOU ARE HERE

↓

was your ex psychologically, emotionally, physically, verbally or financially abusive? is there a power imbalance in the relationship?

NO

YES

↓

YOU CAN TRY MEDIATION OR COLLABORATIVE FAMILY LAW

→

START WITH A LAWYER AND CONSIDER A COURT APPLICATION

What are my options to get a resolution?

I'm glad you asked

1. MEDIATION
2. COLLABORATIVE FAMILY LAW
3. ARBITRATION
4. MED-ARB
5. NEGOTIATION
6. COURT

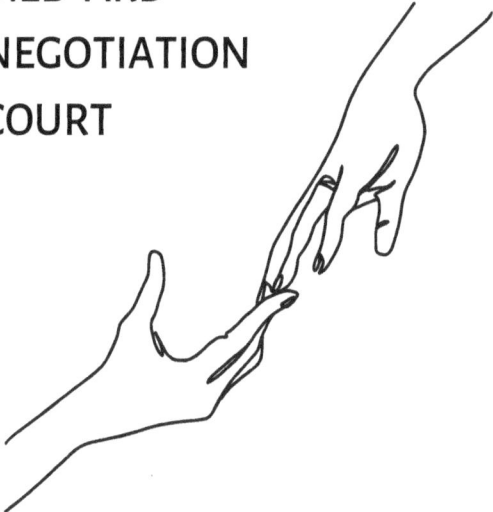

MEDIATION

What is mediation? Part 1

Mediation is a private process whereby you and your ex mutually retain the services of an objective third-party mediator educated in family law and alternative dispute resolution (ADR) to help you arrive at an an
out-of-court solution.

The mediator's job is to identify the issues, ask you and your ex for relevant information, ensure that you exchange the relevant documents, and help you find a mutually acceptable resolution.

You can retain lawyers from the beginning, or you can wait until the end of the process, but be aware -
if your mediator misses an issue that your lawyers catch later on, it can be more expensive, or even fatal to the negotiations, to try to fix it after the fact.

Remember: no matter how friendly they appear, the mediator does not represent you and your interests. They are a neutral third party.

MEDIATION

What is mediation? Part 2

For mediation to function effectively, you and your ex must be committed to resolving issues fairly.

There cannot be a history of abuse, serious mental health issues, or drug abuse impacting either party's ability to be rational.

Abusers can and will delay the process to financially and emotionally exhaust their ex. This can be done to force you into their desired settlement, or to show you they are still in control, or both.

Mediators are supposed to be trained to catch these situations, but sometimes they don't.

If you and your ex are able to resolve the issues with your mediator's help, your mediator will create a document called a **"Memorandum of Understanding"** to outline your agreement in principle.

This document is not binding - you will need it to be transformed into a **Separation Agreement** by your lawyers, and to properly execute it, for it to have legal effect.

MEDIATION

What is mediation? Part 3

In many cases folks are unrepresented until they get to this point. Their mediator will hand them the Memo and tell them to contact separate lawyers to get **independent legal advice** ("ILA").

You and your ex will retain your own lawyers to review the Memo. If issues were missed, or if you no longer agree after obtaining ILA, your lawyers can try to help you negotiate a resolution.

This is a situation to avoid if at all possible! You may have compromised on a difficult issue earlier, thinking you were dealing with all of the relevant topics. It is tough to reopen a "resolved" issue late in the process. This is why it is extremely important to ensure all relevant issues are included from the start.

After this, one lawyer will prepare a **Separation Agreement** in the proper form, and send it to the other party or their lawyer for comment and revision. When you and your ex agree on a draft, your lawyers will assist you both to **execute it** to give it legal effect.

In some cases - for example if support is involved - the executed Separation Agreement may need to be filed with the court using the proper paperwork.

SEPARATION
AGREEMENTS

According to s. 54 of the **Family Law Act** R.S.O. 1990. a Separation Agreement is a domestic contract in which separated parties can agree on their respective rights and obligations, including,

(a) ownership in or division of property;

(b) support obligations;

(c) the right to direct the education and moral training of their children;

(d) the right to decision-making responsibility or parenting time with respect to their children; and

(e) any other matter in the settlement of their affairs.

WARNING:

Do not use a template you found online and assume you're fine. There is no guarantee that the template reflects the law in your jurisdiction, newer amendments to the law, or the issues in your case.

I refuse to provide ILA on Separation Agreements that were not prepared by a competent lawyer as it is simply too risky for me to do so, and it is too risky for my client to use one.

MEDIATION

What is mediation? Part 4

Please note: either you or your ex may choose to waive ILA, but beware - if either of you waives ILA and the Agreement is flawed, based on inadequate disclosure, or improperly negotiated, it could be set aside by a court in the future.

If your ex is:

- threatening you;
- pressuring you to agree to terms you don't understand or have not obtained ILA on;
- pressuring you to agree to terms you don't want;
- insisting on a term but claiming they won't make you follow it later;
- or if you feel obligated to sign because they are threatening that they are going to cut off financial support, harm you or the children, etc.

If you are experiencing **undue influence** also known as **coercion**. This is against the law. You should not sign.

If you or your ex sign under coercion, your Separation Agreement could later be set aside by a Judge. However, this will require you to start a court case and can be costly.

Avoid the expense and headache by consulting with a competent lawyer early on. If you already have a lawyer, tell them honestly what is going on.

COLLABORATIVE FAMILY LAW

What is collaborative family law?

Collaborative family law (CFL) a.k.a. *family dispute resolution* a.k.a. *collaborative practice* is a relatively new family-law specific form of ADR.

In CFL, both you and your ex are represented by lawyers throughout the process, but you all start with the agreement that if you are unable to reach a resolution, you cannot use these lawyers in court.

In order to practice CFL, your lawyer needs special training and membership in the **Ontario Association of Collaborative Professionals.**

You will need to work closely and collaboratively with your ex, their lawyer, and other professionals to reach milestones and goals throughout the process.

You will meet with your lawyer solo, then meet together with your ex and their lawyer to work toward your settlement objectives as a group. Your lawyers will create a safe space to assist you to resolve conflicts. By the end of the process, all agreements will be incorporated into a Separation Agreement.

In an ideal world, CFL allows you and your ex to resolve issues amicably, ending the relationship with respect, and setting you up to co-parent effectively in the future.

COLLABORATIVE FAMILY LAW

Your collaborative lawyers may recommend that you retain accounting, parenting or other professionals to obtain recommendations. In some cases, they may suggest you bring in an effective mediator to help resolve tough issues.

At the risk of stating the obvious, keep in mind that additional professionals = additional cost.

When not to use collaborative family law:

For CFL to work effectively, both parties must be committed to a fair resolution. There cannot be an unbalanced power dynamic for the reasons outlined in the mediation section.

If your ex digs their heels in on issues, this may not be the route for you. It can be challenging to reign in unreasonable parties using CFL.

If either you or your ex lose trust in the CFL process and decide to go to court instead, you will both need to retain new lawyers. Your new lawyers will need money retainers and time to review your files, familiarize themselves with your cases, and request missing disclosure. They will also need to prepare your court materials. This will add cost.

The idea is that this will recommit you to the CFL process unless it is absolutely not going to work for you.

COLLABORATIVE FAMILY LAW

You know your ex better than anyone.

Think about their past actions rather than their past promises.

If you do not trust them to treat you fairly, and to be truly collaborative, do not choose CFL.

ARBITRATION

What is family arbitration? Part 1

Arbitration is an ADR process that allows you and your
ex to tell your story to a neutral, third party arbitrator
in a direct and private setting.

The arbitrator will listen to both of you, find fact,
and make a binding decision.

**Think of the arbitrator as an efficient personal Judge
on a private retainer funded by you and your ex.**

You and your ex <u>must</u> both get independent legal advice
before an arbitrator will work with you. You will need to
agree on the topics that the arbitrator is empowered
to decide before the arbitration begins in a contract
called an **Arbitration Agreement.**

You may have your lawyers represent you at the
arbitration, or you may represent yourself. If
you can afford lawyers, use lawyers.

A good arbitrator is educated in the applicable family law,
will make their decision on a legal basis, and provide
reasons for their decision, just as a Judge would.
Their decision is called an "**award.**"

ARBITRATION

Arbitration is attractive for folks who want flexibility in the process, the privacy of keeping their affairs out of the court system, and a fast-track to a resolution.

While a private arbitrator does come at an expense, it may save you money in the long run by eliminating needless court proceedings and delay.

The up-front price of an arbitrator can be a deterrent, but many regret not giving it serious consideration after spending much more in the court process without reaching a resolution.

The **Alternative Dispute Resolution Institute of Ontario** maintains a list of accredited mediators and arbitrators for you to consider. You may wish to review this list and to make inquiries as to cost before making a decision.

You may also hire a professional for a **med-arb,** where they mediate the issues first, and decide the outstanding issues. This will give you and your ex an opportunity to personalize the outcome as much as possible, with the certainty of a binding decision on the topics you can't agree on.

ARBITRATION

Your arbitrator is empowered to make decisions on property settlement, child support and section 7 expenses, custody and parenting time, spousal support, and other items.

Your arbitrator <u>cannot</u> make a Divorce Order, annulment, restraining, non-harassment or parentage order. You will need to go to court to get these forms of relief.

If there is a history of domestic violence, inform your lawyer and arbitrator. Arbitration may or may not be right for you.

In situations involving a risk of further violence or escalation, talk to a lawyer immediately. You <u>must</u> seriously consider court, where measures can be taken to provide for your physical safety.

So let's talk about retaining a lawyer, and how they can help you try to reach a resolution both in and out of court.

Legal Aid Lawyer

Depending on your income, you may qualify for **legal aid**. Contact **Legal Aid Ontario** to see if you qualify.

Private Retainer

Otherwise, you will be looking at privately retaining a lawyer. You will need to sign a **Retainer Agreement** that outlines the terms of your contract, and pay a money retainer before they start working on your behalf.

Lawyers earn money based off of the time they spend on your file. Most lawyers will keep track of that time to the closest 6 minute interval, and bill you periodically on that basis. Most will require you to pay a money retainer before doing work on your behalf. This is to guarantee that they will be paid for their work. They will also charge you for disbursements, i.e. expenses they incur on your behalf.

Family lawyers are not allowed to take cases on *contingency* i.e. by receiving a percentage of your settlement. If a lawyer is unaware of this rule, or willing to break it, they are demonstrating competency and ethical issues, and you may be better off finding someone else.

However, some lawyers may be willing to *defer payment* for example, if money is coming from the sale of a property like the matrimonial home, or if you have grounds for a motion for **interim disbursements** (where your ex is ordered to front you money for legal fees).

Limited Scope Retainer

If you cannot afford a lawyer on a private retainer, many offer a limited scope retainer whereby they "unbundle" various services.

For example, you can hire them for parts of the work, like legal and case strategy, material preparation, court attendances, motion arguments, and representing you at a trial.

Self-Representation

It can be very difficult to maintain objectivity in your own court case, especially in an emotional area like family law.

If you value your sanity, avoid self-representing at all costs. The system is extremely complex and if you do not understand the law, how to perform certain steps, or if you do something incorrectly, you may lose on a big issue.

Saying that you didn't understand because you are self-represented is not a good excuse. Self-representation is seen as a choice and ignorance of the law is no defence.

If you absolutely must self-represent, consider consulting with a lawyer at various stages throughout the process to make sure you are taking sensible positions, completing your paperwork correctly and representing yourself effectively in court.

HOT TIP

If you have a court attendance and you are unrepresented (haven't had a chance to retain a lawyer) or self-represented, arrive right when the court house opens, find the Duty Counsel, and ask to be placed on their list for free legal advice.

Duty Counsel are qualified lawyers hired by Legal Aid Ontario to provide free legal advice as an emergency "triage" service for anyone on the court docket who needs help.

They are often quite busy, so arriving early is important.

lawyer up

Negotiating a Settlement with a Family Lawyer

If you experienced any form of abuse, lack of respect, or power imbalance in your marriage or common law partnership, retain a court-ready family lawyer from the outset.

Schedule consultations with a few lawyers in your area to find someone you trust and get along with.

Tell them what happened in full, even if you are embarrassed. They can't help you unless they have the truth. They are also bound by the rules of solicitor-client privilege not to reveal anything you say, except with your permission for the purposes of litigation.*

Some lawyers will tell you that infidelity and domestic violence are irrelevant once the relationship is over. This is not true. Beware these lawyers - they are not aware of the new tort of family violence, they don't understand how abuse impacts the other relevant issues, and they may not be able to help you or your children effectively.

*note - if you reveal unreported child abuse or a severe risk to public safety your lawyer may be obligated to report

lawyer up

As discussed, there are penalties for family violence in the Ontario family court system. There is no penalty for cheating; however, a broad series of relevant family issues flow from situations involving infidelity and family violence:

Custodial and parenting time issues:

- Did your child witness or experience violence?
- Did you ex expose your child to adult issues?
- Is your child afraid of your ex?
- Does your ex's parenting time need to be suspended?
- Does it need to be reduced or supervised?
- Is there an active Restraining Order?
- How will that impact exchanges?
- Has your child's mental health been impacted?
- Do they have poor self esteem? Need therapy?
- Is your ex blocking therapy?
- Are you afraid your ex will harm your child?

Support issues:

Have you developed a mental or physical health condition that impacts your ability to work to support yourself?

lawyer up

Remember how I mentioned that if you are ill or unwell you need to get diagnosed by a medical professional?

Q: Why do you need a diagnosis and medical records?

A: It's important to get help, but it is also important to create an ongoing paper trail to prove your claims.

Medical and therapy records that refer to the abuse are a form of proof that the abuse occurred. They will support your claim for tort damages. If the abuse caused a medical or mental health condition that impacted your ability to work, these records will support your claim for spousal support.

If your lawyer cuts you off when you try to talk about abuse, beware. They may not be aware of recent developments in the tort law and they are clearly failing to consider how these situations impact your custody, residence and support claims.

If you are a survivor, you will save yourself a lot of invalidation by finding a trauma-informed lawyer.

lawyer up

Once you have found a lawyer you trust, you will sign a **Retainer Agreement** as previously discussed. It will set out the terms of your lawyer-client relationship.

If any provision confuses or concerns you, you may bring it to another lawyer for review before you sign.

So you have retained a family lawyer you trust:

Congratulations! Now let me demystify the process by listing the typical steps we take from here:

Most lawyers will begin the negotiation process by writing a letter to your ex to advise that they have been retained, and to ask to exchange the relevant financial disclosure within a particular timeline.

Check out s. 21(1) of the *Children's Law Reform Act* to see what we generally exchange.

If your ex delays, threatens you, or talks to your children about legal issues, tell your lawyer. They cannot contact you directly about legal issues after you have retained counsel.

If the other side plays games with disclosure, that is a good, early sign to go to court instead.

financial disclosure

Quick Diversion

Take a moment to review the financial disclosure obligations outlined in the relevant legislation.

If your claim involves **child support**, you must comply with the disclosure requirements under **section 21** of the *Child Support Guidelines* O. Reg 391/97

If your claim involves **child support, spousal support, or a property settlement,** you must comply with **Rule 13** of the *Family Law Rules* O. Reg. 114/99

Look them up online and familiarize yourself with your disclosure obligations.

GOING TO COURT

How to start a court proceeding:

If your ex is unwilling to negotiate in a timely fashion,
your lawyer will need to prepare materials to begin or
defend a family court proceeding.

Don't let the idea of court scare you. Difficult, authoritarian
and controlling exes need the supervision of a Judge
in order to comply with disclosure requirements
and other Orders.

Settlement discussions can and do proceed in parallel
to court as we uncover new information and determine
the strength of each person's case.

99% of matters settle before trial.

In a family law case, the originating process is called
an "**Application**" and it is defended with an "**Answer.**"
If your ex raises new issues in the Answer, you may
file a "**Reply.**" All forms are available online at
ontariocourtforms.on.ca

If you have been to court or filed an executed Separation
Agreement before, you will start this court proceeding with a
"**Motion to Change**" and defend with a "**Response to Motion
to Change.**" However, you will need to show a "**material
change in circumstances**" since the
Final Order or Agreement.

GOING TO COURT

Your lawyer will interview you over one or more appointments in order to understand your case. Your lawyer will also ask you to compile and provide a series of relevant documents.

In addition to your originating process (Application or Motion to Change) you will need to complete a **Financial Statement** (Form 13 if there are support issues; Form 13.1 if there are support and/or property issues), plus a Form 35.1 **Affidavit in Support of Claim for Custody or Access** if you are seeking decision-making or parenting time of a child.

The Financial Statement needs to be as accurate as possible. It will need to be sworn and filed with all relevant financial documents attached.

The Affidavit needs to outline details regarding your child(ren) and your parenting plan, including your plan for contact with the other parent. It's important to show a reasonable plan for contact with the other parent unless you can show they are unsafe.

Your lawyer will then prepare your materials, have you execute them in front of a **Commissioner of Oaths** proving it is truly you who started the case, and then get them issued by the court. This is when you will receive your court file number.

GOING TO COURT

Did you know that there are three types of family court in Ontario?

OCJ   SCJ   Unified

If you were not legally married, or if you are not dealing with property issues, you can file in the **Ontario Court of Justice.**

If you were legally married and you are seeking property relief or a Divorce Order, you must file in the **Superior Court of Justice.**

In some jurisdictions, these courts have been combined into a singular **"Unified Family Court"** which can deal with all issues.

If you are not sure which court to file in, consult with a lawyer.

GOING TO COURT

Once your materials have been issued, your lawyer will retain a **process server** to serve them via **special service** on your ex. This will incur a cost. The easier the service, the lower the cost. If your ex avoids service, this will increase the cost. However, they will look bad to the court in the long run.

<u>You cannot serve your ex yourself.</u> If you try to serve your ex yourself, your documents will not be accepted by the court.

Your ex must be personally served by a third party with no interest in the case. Your process server will swear an **Affidavit of Service** detailing how your ex was served. Your lawyer will then file the materials with the court.

The Affidavit of Service is important because the court must be certain that your ex is aware of this **"originating process"** (new court case). Inaction on their part can lead to legal consequences, such as being **Noted in Default** which will allow you to proceed to an **Uncontested Trial** and to obtain a Final Order in their absence.

Issuing, filing and paying filing fees is now done electronically using the Ontario gov "OneKey" service.

GOING TO COURT

If your ex lives in Canada, they have **thirty (30) days** after service to file their responding court materials.
If they live abroad, they have **sixty (60) days**.

Your ex <u>will not</u> need to retain a process server to serve you with their responding materials. They can email, fax, mail, courier or deposit the documents via electronic document exchange.

They will need to include their own sworn Financial Statement with attachments and Form 35.1 Affidavit in their responding materials.

Once your materials have been exchanged, you will both need to attend a **Mandatory Information Session** on separate dates to learn about court process.
The professional running the session will provide you with a **Completion Certificate** to file with the court.

After this, your lawyers may attempt to negotiate a resolution out of court, or set a first court date.

Keep in mind this book can only provide a high-level overview of steps and rules.

Review the **_Family Law Rules_** _O. Reg. 114/99_ for detailed explanations of the steps involved in the family court process.

ONE LAST TIME

There is no substitute for full legal representation,
but in an imperfect world, a good lawyer on a
Limited Scope Retainer can really
make a difference.

It is worth asking if your lawyer of choice is willing
to help you on this basis rather than going it alone.

If you can't afford a lawyer now, you can retain
one mid-way through your court case.

Keep in mind, if you retain counsel late, **they may
not be able to reverse a bad outcome from
before their time on the case**.

Consider this very seriously.

WHAT'S NEXT?

Next, I will outline the different type of court dates you
may need to attend before getting to a trial.

This will help demystify what happens
at court attendances.

It will also help you understand why
clients sometimes ask:

"why is the Judge doing that?"

BASIC FAMILY COURT CASE STRUCTURE

Case Conference

Motion

Settlement Conference

Trial Management Conference

Trial

These are the types of court appearances in the order they generally occur, except that motions can take place any time after the first Case Conference and before the Trial Management Conference.

We will discuss the types of attendances in greater detail in the following pages.

CASE CONFERENCE

Generally speaking, the first time you will go to court will be for a **Case Conference.**

This is a settlement-style attendance where the Judge is only empowered to make orders you agree with.

Family Law Rule 17(4) states that the purposes of a Case Conference are as follows:

(a) exploring the chances of settling the case;

(b) identifying the issues that are in dispute and those that are not in dispute;

(c) exploring ways to resolve the issues in dispute;

(d) ensuring disclosure of the relevant evidence, including the financial information required to resolve any support or property issue;

(d.1) identifying issues relating to expert evidence or reports the parties intend to rely on at trial;

(e) noting admissions that may simplify the case;

(f) setting the date for the next step in the case;

(g) setting a specific timetable for the steps to be taken in the case before it comes to trial;

(h) organizing a settlement conference, or holding one if appropriate;

...next page

CASE CONFERENCE

(i) giving directions regarding any intended motion, including a specific timetable for the exchange of material and filing of argument summaries, if needed;

(j) in the case of a motion to change a final order or agreement under rule 15, determining the most appropriate process for reaching a quick and just conclusion of the motion.

What to do before the Case Conference?

Both sides will need to prepare, exchange and file **Case Conference Briefs** and updated Financial S tatements, and **confirm** the attendance in accordance with the *Family Law Rules*.

What happens at the Case Conference?

A Judge at a Case Conference may try to settle aspects of the matter by encouraging both sides to see where they are in agreement.

If the parties are too far apart, the Judge may focus on moving the matter forward by encouraging the parties to agree on necessary procedural orders.

Judges do not respond well to conflict at a Case Conference. They will not read your briefs to see who is "right" and who is "wrong" because they are not allowed to find fact at these attendances.

Instead, they will try to understand both sides, and suggest potential compromises on hot issues, or procedural orders to move the matter forward.

CASE CONFERENCE

If you don't agree with the Judge's suggestions at the Case
Conference, you do not have to consent to any
of the orders they suggest.

The most common question after a Case Conference:

**Why did the Judge believe my ex when I have
evidence that they are not telling the truth?**

As previously mentioned, the Judge is not empowered to
decide who they believe at a Case Conference. As a result,
they take each party's statements at face value and treat
them both as though their concerns may be true. Folks
sometimes misinterpret this as meaning that the Judge
believes their ex. Don't fall into this trap, and don't let it get
you down.

At the end of your Case Conference, the Judge will write out
an "Endorsement" outlining the orders that have been
made on consent, and explaining what
the next step will be.

Depending on the specific facts of your case, the next steps
are usually one of the following:

- A **"To Be Spoken To"** (a quick check-in; used when
  the court needs an update before the next date
  can be set);
- a second Case Conference;
- a Settlement Conference if the Judge thinks you   will
  be ready to meaningfully discuss settlement; or
- a motion to get an order on a contested issue.

SETTLEMENT CONFERENCE

Now let's talk about the purposes of a
Settlement Conference.

Family Law Rule 17(5) states that the purposes of a
Settlement Conference are as follows:

(a) exploring the chances of settling the case;

(b) settling or narrowing the issues in dispute;

(c) ensuring disclosure of the relevant evidence;

(c.1) settling or narrowing any issues relating to any expert
evidence or reports on which the parties intend to rely at
trial;

(d) noting admissions that may simplify the case;

(e) if possible, obtaining a view of how the court might
decide the case;

(f) considering any other matter that may help in a quick
and just conclusion of the case;

(g) if the case is not settled, identifying the witnesses and
other evidence to be presented at trial, estimating the time
needed for trial and scheduling the case for trial;

(h) organizing a trial management conference, or holding
one if appropriate; and

(i) in the case of a motion to change a final order or
agreement under rule 15, determining the most
appropriate process for reaching a quick and just
conclusion of the motion.

SETTLEMENT CONFERENCE

You will both need to prepare, exchange and file **Settlement Conference Briefs** and updated Financial Statements before this attendance. You will also need to **confirm** the attendance.

This is another settlement-style attendance. The Judge is not empowered to make orders unless both sides agree.

However, at a Settlement Conference, **the Judge will offer their opinion** of each party's likelihood of success at a trial.

This is done to encourage the parties to settle in accordance with the strength of their respective cases rather than going forward to a trial.

The parties can craft a settlement personalized to their situation. You may have to compromise in places, but you will save money, time and uncertainty.

That said, if the parties are not willing to consent to a partial or full resolution, the Judge cannot impose an outcome on anyone.

At the end of a Settlement Conference, the Judge may schedule the next attendance, from the following options:

- a "To Be Spoken To";
- a second Settlement Conference;
- a motion; or
- a Trial Management Conference.

...let's talk about what a motion is next

MOTION

Either party may make a motion to the court at any time after a Case Conference on the substantive issues has been held.

A **motion** is a mini-trial on one or more issues that will allow the court to make:

1. A temporary order;
2. Directions on how to carry on the case; or
3. A change in a temporary order.

The parties must co-operate to obtain a date and schedule for exchange of motion materials.

The parties will outline what they are asking the court for in a **Notice of Motion** with written evidence provided in one of more sworn **Affidavits**.

Motions may be characterized as "short" or "long" depending on the length of the materials and estimated argument. Motions are complex and depend on the facts of the case.

You will need to follow the *Family Law Rules*, *Notices to the Profession* and the *Practice Directions* for the specific region in which you reside in order to make sure that your motion is heard.

You will need to argue your case at the motion, making reference to your materials. The Judge is empowered to find fact and make one or more temporary Orders, including for costs.

TRIAL MANAGEMENT CONFERENCE

Rule 17(6) of the *Family Law Rules* states that the purposes of a **Trial Management Conference** include:

(a) exploring the chances of settling the case;

(b) arranging to receive evidence by a written report, an agreed statement of facts, an affidavit or another method, if appropriate;

(c) deciding how the trial will proceed;

(c.1) exploring the use of expert evidence or reports at trial, including the timing requirements for service and filing of experts' reports;

(d) ensuring that the parties know what witnesses will testify and what other evidence will be presented at trial;

(e) estimating the time needed for trial; and

(f) setting the trial date, if not already been done.

If your case is in the Ontario Court of Justice (OCJ), you will exchange **Trial Management Conference Briefs** on the schedule outlines in the *Family Law Rules*.

If your case is in the SCJ or Unified Family Court (also referred to as the *Family Court of the Superior Court of Justice*), you will need to exchange **Trial Scheduling Endorsement Forms, Offers to Settle**, and draft **Opening Statements** for Trial, among other things.

OTHER TYPES OF ATTENDANCES

In urgent situations, a party may be able to bring an **emergency motion** before having a Case Conference.

In rare situations, a motion may be brought to court *ex-parte*, i.e. without notice to the other side. (For example, I once won an *ex parte* **motion** to prevent a baby from being circumcised by an unsafe doctor.)

There are also out-of-court processes that may be required. For example, a **Questioning** is an examination under oath at a court reporter's office where the parties are cross-examined by opposing counsel.

If the matter proceeds to trial, your answers at the Questioning could be brought up on the stand to show a discrepancy in your evidence then and now, and to undermine your credibility.

If you are a survivor of domestic violence, and if you have mental health or memory issues as a result, a **trauma-informed lawyer** could make all the difference in preparing your case, and in preparing you.

Many other possible variations of attendances may come into play in your case. It is impossible to predict. Each type of attendance has specific rules around it that you must follow. We did not have time or space to get into all of it here.

There is no substitute for specific legal advice based on your unique situation.

MAKING OFFERS TO SETTLE

The Ontario family court system encourages parties to settle.

One way is by mandating settlement-style attendances, like Case Conferences and Settlement Conferences before a Trial of the matter is allowed.

Another way is by requiring a Case Conference to take place before a motion in most situations.

A third way is by giving parties inventives for making reasonable offers, like requiring the other side to pay your legal costs if they don't accept.

According to Rule 18(14) of the **Family Law Rules**, your ex may have to pay part of the **legal costs** you incurred up to the date the offer was served, and your **full recovery costs** from that date forward as long as:

1. If the offer relates to a motion, it is made at least one day before the motion date;
2. If the offer relates to a trial it is made at least. seven days before the trial;
3. The offer does not expire and is not withdrawn before the hearing starts;
4. The offer is not accepted; and
5. The party who made the offer obtains an order that. is as favourable as or more favourable than the offer.

There are other rules, for example around proper form and service of the offer, that you must follow. Read the Rule in its entirety for more detail.

You made it!

Good job. I know that was a lot.

The overview that we have just completed is general and every bit will not apply to all cases.

However, it should give you enough information to understand the options open to you, and to advocate for yourself with legal professionals.

Next, we will cover the ways that you can save money by preparing in advance of legal appointments.

STEP FOUR

collecting the relevant information

COLLECT
INFORMATION

Legal time is **_the_** major litigation expense.

If you are able to reduce your lawyer's time on your file, you will save money.

This section is designed to assist you to collect the information that your lawyer will require in order to reduce the time they will need to spend on your case.

What if you're just contemplating separation?
We will outline the evidence to collect to develop a strong case before you leave.

What if you are already separated? Then we will outline the additional evidence you will need to collect to put together the strongest case possible.

COLLECT
INFORMATION
so you're thinking about leaving...

COLLECT
INFORMATION

Open a word processor and begin to write out answers to the questions outlined on the following pages (digital is important as your lawyer can cut and paste, which saves time and may reduce legal fees).

Create a "family law" folder on your computer in which you can organize and save the relevant documents. Go back and re-read the last section - compile all the documents you can.

Create a physical folder for any original physical documents that you will need to compile, for example, your original Marriage Certificate, prior Divorce Order, or Certificate of Divorce.

If you are experiencing abuse, create these files on a password protected personal device that your abuser cannot access.

DON'T LIE

As you compile information, make sure to tell the truth.

If you cannot settle, you will have to resort to court. Consider taking reasonable positions, or else you will not settle, and you will spend a lot more in legal fees.

Decision-makers will assess your credibility. Most Judges believe that there is a continuum in the truth and that one of you is closer to it. It is their job to "find" the fact between your versions of events. If you are able to tell the truth with evidence to back it up, the Judge is more likely to find in your favour.

You cannot participate in court process while doing illegal things like lying to the court. We use the metaphor of "clean hands" - **you cannot come to the court with unclean hands and ask for a favour**.

The law will not respect you, unless you respect it.

Many lawyers will fire you as a client if you lie to them. They do not want to represent someone who will have them lie to a Judge.

Family court is (hopefully) something you will face only once in your life. Lawyers are there every day, and they will not ruin their reputation for one client.

COLLECT INFORMATION

1.   Proof of custody and/or family violence claims:

Show how much you were involved with the kids; how little your partner was involved; how your partner treated you; how they treated the kids; outline the harm they caused you and the kids if any; and other things specific to your situation with this evidence:

(a) photos, videos, screen shots, & screen captures;

(b) video captures of text or message exchanges (use your phone's voice-to-text function to transcribe and format them so they are easier for your lawyer to read and use, and provide both);

(c) records proving your parenting involvement:

- medical records showing you made and attended appointments with the kids;
- educational records showing you were involved with the school, attended parent/teacher conferences, school trips, PTA, etc;
- proof you arranged babysitting or daycare;
- proof you facilitated extra-curriculars; and

(e) copies of police records, CAS records, witness statements, etc.

shield the children

Your responsibility as a parent is to shield your children from adult issues. The court takes this very seriously.

Do not discuss legal issues with your children.

Do not record them for use in litigation.

Do not coach them against your spouse.

Do not ask them on camera to relate alleged instances of abuse or bad behaviour
by your spouse.

These actions are harmful to children and
Judges have zero tolerance for this.

If you need to determine the child's point of view, you can ask the Judge for an Order asking the **Office of the Children's Lawyer (OCL)** to get involved.

The OCL is a taxpayer-funded service that provides children with a voice in litigation. If the child is too young to give instructions, a trained social worker will be assigned to ascertain what it in their best interest. Otherwise, your child will be assigned a lawyer they can speak to directly.

If the OCL declines to get involved, you can hire one of their panelists privately for a **"section 30 assessment" under the** *Children's Law Reform Act.*

IF YOU ARE CURRENTLY EXPERIENCING FAMILY VIOLENCE:

If your spouse is abusive toward the children, or toward you in the children's presence, your obligation is to **report the abuse** to the proper authorities.

If you are experiencing an emergency, call the **police** emergency line, 9-1-1.

If you are not in immediate danger, contact a **domestic violence shelter** or your local **Children's Aid Society** to report the abuse and establish an exit plan.

These organizations have resources to help you, including lawyers on staff. They may be able to help you document the abuse and plan your exit without harming your children or your case.

COLLECT
INFORMATION

If you are contemplating leaving, collect the following information & documents in a safe place:

2. **Proof of income** – *was your partner in control of the finances? If so, you may not have access to your records after you leave.*

Collect full copies of your income and tax documents including:

- contract/letter of employment;
- your personal Income Tax Returns for the last three years;
- Notices of Assessment and/or Reassessment for the last three years;
- T4, T4A, T5 documents;
- three recent pay stubs;
- Statement of Earnings if you are self-employed;
- Proof of short or long-term disability income, EI, WSIB income, ODSP or OW income

Consult with a lawyer to see if you can keep copies of *your spouse's income documents*, if they were shared with you during marriage. Ask if you are allowed to collect evidence of any under-the-table cash work your spouse engaages in as they may try to hide this income post-separation.

COLLECT INFORMATION

If you are contemplating leaving, collect the following information & documents in a safe place:

3. **Financial evidence** - *collect documents proving the value of assets and debts at marriage and at present, including but not limited to*:

- Agreement of Purchase and Sale & Statement of Adjustments for any real property (matrimonial home, income property, cottage, etc);

- mortgage, leasing and financing documents;

- sale contracts for vehicles, leisure vehicles, collections, and other major assets;

- appraisals for assets, vehicles and valuable collections;

- copies of all bank account, investment account, and credit facility statements for the last three years (don't forget crypto, pensions, air miles, credit card points etc);

- leases for any rental properties owned jointly, individually, or by a third party for your interest;

- incorporation papers for any businesses, business name registration documents, general ledgers, statements of income, annual reports, copies of contracts, proof of expenses;

- Anything else of relevance to your situation.

PROTECT YOUR ASS(ETS)

If you are considering leaving, there are steps you can take to protect certain types of assets.

For example, an **inheritance** or **personal injury damages award** made in your name (not naming your spouse) is generally considered "**excluded property.**"

This means that your spouse is not entitled to a share in it unless you introduce it into the shared family property.

<u>**Do not**</u> turn a house you inherit into a *matrimonial home* by living in it together as a primary residence unless you want your spouse to own half.

<u>**Do not**</u> take an *inheritance* or cash traceable to the inheritance and put it in a joint bank account, or use it to pay down the mortgage on the matrimonial home or another joint debt, unless you want your spouse to own half.

If you have money or a major asset coming to you, consult with a family lawyer ASAP to make sure that you don't do something that gives half of it away to a spouse you are thinking about leaving.

I left. Now what do I do?

...now it's time to identify the issues and compile the rest of the evidence in support of your claims.

WISH LIST

Check off all the relief you think you need:

- Divorce?
- Support for me?
- Support for child(ren)?
- Decision-making responsibility for children?
- Parenting time with child(ren) – how would you suggest that parenting time be split? Why?
- Contact with child(ren)? (if you are not allowed contact upload related documents and explain)
- Restraining or non-harassment order?
- Have you or the other party been criminally charged? (upload related documents)
- Indexing spousal support?
- Declaration of parentage? (DNA testing)
- Guardianship over child's property?
- Wrongful removal or retention of child in Ontario?
- Equalization of net family property?
- Exclusive possession of matrimonial home?
- Exclusive possession of contents of matrimonial home?
- Freezing assets?
- Sale of family property?
- Unjust enrichment?
- Costs?
- Annulment of marriage?
- Prejudgment interest?

COLLECT
INFORMATION

First, you will need to collect info about yourself:

- Your full legal name:
- Date of birth:
- Your phone number, address and email address:
- Where you live: (municipality); (province)
- Employment for the last three (3) years:
- Income in the last three (3) years:
- Your name immediately before marriage:
- Other names you have been known by:
- Gender before marriage: (M); (F); (another gender)?
- Married before? Y or N
- If yes: date of first marriage? Date of divorce order? Do you have a copy? Y or N
- Location of previous divorce?

Documents:

Upload your three (3) most recent personal Income Tax Returns, Notices of Assessment/Reassessment, and pay stubs, as well as your T4(s) for last year if your taxes are not yet done, and any other docs outlined in the legislation outlined in the financial disclosure section.

If you have a copy of your Marriage Certificate, Divorce Order, or Certificate of Divorce, scan copies and set aside your originals.

COLLECT INFORMATION

Now, you will need to compile info about your ex:

- Their full legal name:
- Date of birth:
- Their email address and physical address:
- Where they live: (municipality); (province)
- Their employment for the last three (3) years:
- Their income in the last three (3) years:
- Their name immediately before marriage:
- Other names they have been known by:
- Gender before marriage: (M); (F); (other)?
- Married before? Y or N
- If yes: date of first marriage?
- Date of divorce order?
- Do you have a copy? Y or N
- Location of previous divorce?

Documents:

Do you have copies of your ex's three (3) most recent personal Income Tax Returns, Notices of Assessment/Reassessment, and pay stubs? Their T4(s) for last year if their taxes are not done? Anything else outlined in the financial disclosure section?

Do you have a copy of your ex's Divorce Order or Certificate of Divorce? If so, scan and upload it.

COLLECT
INFORMATION

Answer the following questions:

Where do you live?

- Where did you live during the relationship?
- Provide the address:
- Do you rent or own?
- If you own, who is named on the deed?
- When did you buy?
- What was the purchase price?
- Do you have an appraisal as of the date of separation?
- Who lives in the home now?

Relationship Dates:

- When did you start cohabiting (living together)?
- When did you marry?
- When did you separate?
- Never lived together? Y or N
- Still living together? Explain:

COLLECT
INFORMATION

**Now provide the following information
about each of your children:**

- Full legal name?
- Child of the relationship? Y or N
- If N, who is the other parent? Is there a Separation Agreement or Final Order? Upload it.
- If Y, what is their age?
- Birth date?
- Where do they live?
- Who are they living with?
- What was their sex at birth?
- What is their sex now?
- What is their gender?
- What are their pronouns?
- Family physician name, address, phone number, email address?
- Other medical specialists? Same info as above.
- Does this child have healthcare needs? If Y, explain?
- Medication? If Y, explain?
- Therapy? If Y explain?
- Do you think this child needs medical attention for an as-yet undiagnosed issue? Y or N; explain.
- Does this child participate in extra-curricular activities?
- If Y, explain, and upload proof of the cost.

COLLECT INFORMATION

**Provide the following information about prior
Final Orders or Agreements:**

Previous Final Order:

Have the parties or children been in a court case before?
If Y, upload a copy of the Final Order and provide:
- Date:
- Judge:
- Court:
- Which paragraphs do you want to change? Why?

Prior Agreement:

Have the parties made a written agreement dealing with
any matter involved in this case?

If yes, upload a copy of the Separation Agreement and
provide:
- Date of execution (date on which latter party signed):
- Name of each party and their lawyer:
- Is there a specific paragraph or provision you are
  disagreeing over?
- If Y, give the paragraph number, write out the
  paragraph language, and explain the disagreement.
- Have you tried to resolve the issue? Explain.

COLLECT INFORMATION

Answer the following questions:

Notice of Calculation:

- Has a Notice of Calculation or Recalculation been issued by the online Child Support Service in this case? Y or N

- If Y: give the date and type of each notice and upload a copy of each;

- If Y: are you asking the court to make an order for child support in a different amount from what is set out in the notice? Y or N; if Y, explain why?

Arbitration:

- Have the parties arbitrated or agreed to arbitrate any matter involved in this case? Y or N

If Y, give the date of the Arbitration Agreement and family arbitration Award if any; upload copies of the Agreement and/or Award

PARENTING
RESPONSIBILITIES

Explain your parenting involvement before and after separation. Here are questions to get you started:

- Who gets up with the kids in the morning?
- What time?
- What needs to be done with the kids to get ready?
- Who makes their lunches? When?
- Where do the kid(s) go during the day? (give details of the school, daycare, relative, babysitter, etc including name, address, and how long the children have been enrolled)
- How do the kid(s) get there?
- Who is responsible if a child is sick in the morning?
- Who is responsible if a child calls sick from school?
- When do the children finish school/daycare/other?
- Who picks them up, how do they get home? Explain:
- Who prepares dinner?
- What is your evening routine?
- Who is responsible for the bedtime routine?
- What is your bathing and hygiene routine?
- Who wakes up with the children at night?
- Who is responsible for facilitating extra-curricular activities?
- Who attends parent/teacher meetings? School functions? Medical appointments? Dental? Optometry? Other specialists?

Provide any other parenting information relevant to your situation and claims.

PARENTING
PLAN

Now write out your **Parenting Plan** for the future, including how you intend to help the children maintain their relationship with your ex and family members on both sides, if appropriate in your situation.
If not, explain why.

Outline where you intend to live, where the children will go to school or daycare, and whether you will maintain or change their educational, medical, dental, optometry, therapeutic care, and other healthcare providers.

Outline whether you will continue to allow them to participate in their current church, spiritual or cultural communities. Explain how.

Will they get to do the same extra-curricular activities? Will you support their existing friendships? Explain.

The more consistency and stability you offer, the more likely the court will side with you.

LIST OF PROPOSED
WITNESSES

Make a **list of potential witnesses** with first person experience of the relevant issues who could assist you to prove your claim.

Write down their full legal name and contact information, along with a paragraph on what topics you think they would be able to testify about.

Consider family members, friends, medical care providers, health care providers, therapists, extra-curricular activity coaches or volunteers, colleagues, co-workers, employers, neighbours, CAS workers, police officers, and others who can speak first-hand to the relevant issues.

your chronology

Now we are at the most important step: you are going to write out a chronology of your relationship. Every notable thing that happened that relates to your claims, from when you started dating to now.

breathe

we are going to do our best not to have a menty b

I know the idea is daunting, but this is going to save you the most money of all. If done well, it will avoid hours of costly lawyer meetings.

chronology

When I left my abuser, I needed to write everything out
to make it external to me so that I could heal. This
exercise will allow you to do the same
and to reduce your legal fees.

Instructions:
Write down everything you remember in order of
what happened. Add in additional details
as you remember them.

Note: if you have been diagnosed with CPTSD or
another mental health issue, or think that you might
have an undiagnosed mental health issue, talk to your
doctor before starting this exercise. Some professionals
think facing your trauma is healing, but others warn it
might be retraumatizing.

Your doctor will advise if this is safe for you.

chronology

Did you know that... when you have been in a stressful situation, the cortisol levels in your system focus your brain on survival, and make it harder to encode long term memories?

This is why some events might be fuzzy and others might be hard to recall. If you are still in the relationship, consider keeping a journal to keep track of what is happening.

Contemporaneous notes are evidence in court.

It will be easy to remember some things, but others will come back as you jog your memory. Fill in gaps in your timeline as you remember them. It usually takes a week or two to get everything down.

Look at the time and date stamps on your texts, photos in your camera roll, or social media accounts to confirm the timeline. Save copies to prove your timeline is accurate.

WHAT TO DO
WITH ALL THIS

When you make your first appointment with your lawyer, send them a copy of your chronology and a link to a folder with the rest of the information you have compiled.

Gmail comes with free cloud storage. Dropbox cloud storage is available for free. You can also send large folders or files using WeTransfer or another secure file transfer service.

Otherwise, you can drop it off at their office in advance of your appointment on a thumb drive.

If you are unable to complete everything outlined, that is okay. I know it's a lot.

Whatever you were able to get down will help your future lawyer.

If you are experiencing an emergency, contact a lawyer right away, even if you have not completed all of the information gathering outlined in this book. **Do not wait.**

INFORMATION?

STEP FIVE

believe a better future is possible

A better future is possible for you, and
I am living proof of it.

I genuinely didn't think I would ever heal, but
with the right care I have, and
you can as well.

I am not a doctor or a therapist, so please keep
that in mind; however, I am a survivor, and I
know what worked for me.

In the following pages I will share some
concepts that helped me to understand what
happened to me, and helped
me begin to heal.

If you are interested in these ideas, use this as
a starting point. Discuss these ideas with your
health care team to start a conversation around
your own healing.

**The first step for me was to understand how
manipulative and abusive people behave:**

Love-bombing - a technique used by abusers to
create intimacy more quickly than normal. They
will tell you that they love you, that you are their
soul mate, or that you are perfect, when they
hardly know you in order to gain control over you
and manipulate your emotions. This preys on the
fantasy of "love at first sight."

Mirroring - a technique whereby the abuser
reflects your behaviours, likes and dislikes, back
at you, to make you trust them, drop
your defences, and fall in love with
them more quickly.

The cycle of abuse - this is a key concept first developed in the late seventies to explain the pattern of abuse and why victims don't leave.

The original version includes four steps:

(1) *Tension building* - tensions increase, the victim becomes fearful and needs to placate the abuser;

(2) *Incident* - the abuser lashes out. This can take many forms including neglect, silent treatment, verbal, physical, psychological, emotional, financial or other abuse;

(3) *Reconciliation* - the abuser apologizes, blames you, says that the abuse was not as bad as it was, or that it never happened;

This step may also include **hoovering**, i.e. love-bombing you to suck you back in, and promising that they will never hurt you again; and

(4) *Calm* - you are back in the honeymoon phase and you are willing to overlook the abuse because you want to believe the abuser who swears it will not happen again.

Gaslighting – a technique used by manipulators and abusers to cause their victims to question their perception of reality. They will directly contradict your memory of experiences to cause you to question yourself, make you more docile, and better able to control.

Future Faking – a technique used by manipulators and abusers whereby they project a "fake" future with you to keep you holding on but never fulfill the promises.

Trauma bonding - a bond that forms due to abuse. It is a surface-level feeling of attachment and intimacy created by the abuse cycle. In a trauma bond, you think you are experiencing true love even though the abuser is hurting you.

Reactive "abuse" - prolonged exposure to abuse can provoke you to respond in an out-of-character way. Those of us who work on increasing abuse awareness recognize that reactivity does occur, but it should not be called "abuse." It is a response to abuse.

**A few ways to deal with emotional and verbal
abusers if you absolutely cannot leave:**

Grey rocking – if someone tries to provoke you,
respond as though you were a grey rock. In other
words, don't react. If you absolutely must give an
answer, make it as short and simple as possible.
Do not engage if they try to provoke you.

The J.A.D.E. technique – piggybacks off of this – do not
Justify, **A**rgue, **D**efend, or **E**xplain yourself. "No" is a full
sentence. This short and simple answer is enough.

This may anger the abuser at first. Please be careful.
Make sure you can remove yourself from the situation
and/or access help if your abuser escalates.

Once you are safe, you may choose to **heal loudly** by
talking about what happened to you. Again, be careful.
Keep in mind that your abuser may claim you are
slandering them. "The truth" is a full defence, but if
they sue you, you will still need resources to
defend the claim in court.

Your safety should always be the first priority.

Other than talk therapy, a good psychiatrist and proper medication, the concept of "golden threads" helped me to transform my life the most.

Golden threads – a technique I used in my own recovery. The idea of "getting better" is overwhelming. It is difficult to know where to start or how.

This is a cognitive behavioural therapy practice that allows you to change your mindset, and by extension your life, a little bit at a time.

Implement "golden threads" of beauty in your daily life. This will look different for everyone.

If you love exercise or the outdoors, take a walk or work out each day. If you love music, spend time listening to your favourite song. If you are social, make time to talk to a friend, or participate in an online community.

Each of these positive experiences will begin to weave golden threads through your days until your life feels rewarding and golden in general.

PRO-TIP: QUIT DRINKING

I know you don't want to hear this.

... but if you are **abusing alcohol or non-prescription drugs**, access supports to cut back or quit.

These substances may help you cope at first but they will harm you in the long-run.

The worst thing about drinking your pain away is that when the buzz wears off, the pain and trauma are still there.

Alcohol and drugs are not a solution. They postpone your problems to tomorrow, and may make them worse.

You are going to have to deal with your problems sometime, so why not today?

The sooner you do, the sooner you can heal and start living your life again.

Thank you for reading - I sincerely hope that this book helps to make separation less scary, and assists you to take control of a resolution, your healing journey, and the rest of your life.

With love and gratitude,

Heather

Heather D. Alexander BAH, MA, JD, is an experienced family lawyer with extensive training in alternative dispute resolution. She is also a survivor of domestic violence..

She was called to the Bar of the Province of Ontario in 2013 after graduating with distinction from Western Law.

She specializes in helping clients avoid future issues by establishing pre-nuts before problems arise, and by negotiating separation agreements out of court after relationships break down.

However, she is also an experienced trial lawyer who has appeared at all levels of the Ontario Courts. She will stand up for your rights in court fearlessly.

Heather's personal mission is to improve the way that survivors of domestic violence are treated in the family court system. In particular, her aim is to improve the judiciary and legal bar's understanding of the realities of psychological and emotional abuse.